W9-BYU-348

Diversifications

By the same author

Ommateum
Expressions of Sea Level
Corsons Inlet
Tape for the Turn of the Year
Northfield Poems
Selected Poems
Uplands
Briefings
Collected Poems: 1951–1971
(winner of the National Book Award for Poetry, 1973)
Sphere: The Form of a Motion
(winner of the 1973–1974 Bollingen Prize in Poetry)

Diversifications

Poems

• •

A. R. AMMONS

W · W · NORTON & COMPANY · INC ·
NEW YORK

Copyright © 1975 by A. R. Ammons
First Edition
All Rights Reserved
Published simultaneously in Canada
by George J. McLeod Limited, Toronto
Library of Congress Cataloging in Publication Data
Ammons, A   R   1926–
    Diversifications.

    Poems.
    I. Title.
PS3501.M6D5   811'.5'4   75–11616
ISBN 0-393-04414-9
ISBN 0-393-04420-3 pbk.
Printed in the United States of America
1 2 3 4 5 6 7 8 9

for Richard Howard

Contents

Acknowledgments

I would like to thank the editors of the following periodicals for first publishing the poems listed:

American Review   "The Marriage"
Antaeus   "Terminations"
Brim   "Uppermost"
Café Solo   "Fix"
Chicago Review   "Narrows"
Diacritics   "Full," "Lightning," "Double Exposure," "Emerson," "Meeting the Opposition," "History," "Tussock," "Fundamental Constant," "Ballad," "Mind," "Attenuations," "Turning"
Epoch   "Transcendence," "Ars Poetica," "80-Proof"
Georgia Review   "Making It"
Granite   "Louise"
Harper's   "Delight"
The Hudson Review   "Pray Without Ceasing"
Modern Occasions   "Salt Flats"
New Letters   "Imago," "Self-Projection," "Certainty"
     New York Quarterly   "Imperialist," "Weight," "Sight Unseen," "Having to Do with Birth"
New York Times   "Currencies," "Appearances," "The Flaw"
Poetry   "Bonus"

Quarterly Review of Literature   "Measure," "Three
    Travelogues"
Raven   "Glass Globe"
Salmagundi   "Insouciance," "Crying Out"

Diversifications

Transcendence

Just because the transcendental,
having digested all change into
a staying, promises foreverness,

it's still no place to go, nothing
having survived there into life:
and here, this lost way, these

illusory hollyhocks and garages,
this is no place to settle: but
here is the grief, at least,

constant, that things and loves
go, and here the love that
never comes except as permanence.

Insouciance

You notice
as
the flowering spike
of the
forget-me-not
lengthens
with flowering it
leaves
behind a drab notation (namely
seeds even
smaller
than the flowers)
which does not
say
forget me not
because
it means to
be back

Narrows

Constrictions, gross substantialities (the lifting
of form) figure definitions: narrows govern seas:
like there at Gibraltar, an enrichment,

landforms, Africa's good-sized mountain easily as if
seeing across the Straits, looking into Iberia, the
Mediterranean touching the Atlantic in a seeable

scape: that ruffling of surfaces, Atlantic weather
mixing with Mediterranean, the winds of each weather
buttressing, reconciling their systems: awareness frantic

with things and differences, the forces of great matters
brought into concisions of resolution: the meeting
of differences, a sexual stir: (I liked it there: I

was amused and somewhat afraid:) strictures clarify:
the rock, coarsened with form, has an edge, at least,
like relief: the mulling ocean, au contraire, seldom

shows an island, whale, or glacier, its mounts of
a watery likeness, however majestically they lift,

roll, suck under, and kill: get at the stone in the

duct, though, and you know why the bladder swells:
bolus in the artery, quickly damaging: but the ocean's
fine, in a way, with a life of its own apart from

inlets and outlets: knots, tangles, twists draw
attention, provide milieu, engrossing turn and contrariety,
give circulations focus, wield greatnesses unspecific:

how can we leave the narrows firm, surveyable, and
prefer undifferentiations' wider motions: how can we
give up control into being controlled: the suasions.

Salt Flats

I need this broad place to work because I'm
    not certain what design wants
to emerge: I have to have room to work in various
places
    with minor forms
      reconciling multiplicity here and there

a little at a time
before unity, subsuming all lesser curves and devices,
    can assume perimeter:
      the blue-air mountains
on the plain's edge jingled with vanishment:

I set to work: here is this, I said, drawing from
    a center certain yearnings into line:
and here is this, wavy: I ran several miles
across the sand, roughed an area off, then
    informed it deeply with glyph and figure:
when
a single wind arrived, set
down its many hands, whirled, and made me out.

Full

I retire from
the broad engagements,
leave the line
and go
back into the woods
to openings of

hillslides and lakes:
I do not want
to be
loud with emptiness
a hundred years
from now: the

simple event
suffices—complete—
when fall
hawkweed spindling
lifts a single
adequate blossom.

Uppermost

The top
grain on the peak
weighs next
to nothing and,
sustained
by a mountain,
has no burden,
but nearly
ready to float,
exposed
to summit wind,
it endures
the rigors of having
no further
figure to complete
and a
blank sky
to guide its dreaming

Lightning

Once a roving man
tired of roving
took a place and
planted a tree

which grew
year by year—
its

roots deepened, complicating,
its
branches filled out

holding, figuring
space:

and the man,
mirrored, stood
in the tree:

one day the causes of
his roving

found him and struck:

he turned to the tree:
it held
and could not go:

tired of roving but
unable to stay,
where could
he go:

he hangs from the tree.

The Marriage

The world is wound round
with theorems, a winding:
syntax in thickets meshing:

coalescences of ongoing
darkening with thread of
thought, unraveling: tangles

of hypothesis weaving
semantic currents: spools
of possibility feeding

spun cotton balls: caps
of *a priori* with zones of
steamy incipience: the mind's

spider laying into the natural
motions binding filaments
of sight, the orb sustaining

warps of motion under
heaving, forced declarations:
ah, this caught thing!

it can't get loose from
meanings and the mind
can't pull free of it.

Self-Portraits

Though I have cut down, pulled up, and
plowed you under, don't, weeds, spurn
my more usual love:
that others have hated you
costs my love not a quality:
because others have hated you
my imagination, at home with dirty
saints, gets sand in its eyes:
if this lessens neither your horror nor mine,
if this lessens neither your hardiness nor mine,
still it adds my pip to the squeak:
the rejected turn strange
to get their song through: I'm familiar
with byways: I've worn
paths out of several unlocated woods.

Double Exposure

Flounder-like, poetry
flattens white
against bottom mud

so farthest tremors can get
full-ranged to the bone:
but on the side it flowers

invisible with blue mud-work
imitations, it
turns both eyes.

Currencies

I participate
with rain:
precipitate at twig-ends

and come
down:
drop from the bellies of galls:

elbows of branches accumulate
trembling nodes
that

flash fang-silver
into
snow-soaked ground:

I participate with
rain's
gathering and coming down:

hear me, gathered into runlets,
brooks, breaking over falls,
escaping with the silver of seeing.

Bonus

The hemlocks slumped
already as if bewailing
the branch-loading

shales of ice, the rain
changes and a snow
sifty as fog

begins to fall, brightening
the ice's bruise-glimmer
with white holdings:

the hemlocks, muffled,
deepen to the grim
taking of a further beauty on.

Emerson

The stone longs for flight,
the flier for a bead, even
a grain, of connective stone:
which is to say, all
flight, of imaginative hope or
fact, takes accuracy from stone:

without the bead the flier
released from
tension has no true
to gauge his motions in:
assured and terrified by
its cold weight, the stone

can feather the thinnest
possibility of height:
that you needed
to get up and I down
leaves us both still
sharing stone and flight.

Meeting the Opposition

The wind sidles up to
and brusquely in a swell flattens
lofting one side
of the spirea bush:
but the leaves have

so many edges, angles
and varying curvatures that
the wind on the other side
seeps out in a
gentle management.

Appearances

I could believe water
is not water
and stone not stone
but when

water comes
down the brook
corresponding with
perfect

accuracy of adjustment
to the brookbed,
spreading like a pane
over slate

or wrinkling into
muscles to skirt
a tilt
or balking

into a deep loss of
direction

behind a tangled dam
and when

I feel those
motions correspond
to my own, my
running quick and

thin and stalling broody,
I think a real
brook and I in some
missing mirror meet.

Measure

for Robert Morgan

I said there must be someway
to determine
what good
a stalk of grass is—what

other measure but man?

In the hierarchy of use
to us
sea-oats are
inconsequential. But since

they exist, they
exist in the measure of
themselves
and promote the measure.

Delight

The angels who in innocent if
not painless intelligence
fly around a lot (sometimes away)

flew down one day
to the pastures of men
and said

"look, this one's a stone
brunted
and there is one turning in himself

like a burnt-over viper
and look, this one's
broader in his eyes than the world"

and the angels grew surprised
with the quantity
of contortion, misplacement, and mischance:

the stone cried
"if I am not to take myself

as I am, by

what means am I to be changed" and the viper
said
"the fountains of myself are a vision

I will not behold" and others grown old in
pain
cried out "who am I"

and the angels said "shall we give advice"
and said "should we
bring water

or bread or should we at least slay
selected ones"
but knowing neither whether to accept

the pastures as they were nor, if not, any
means to change them
veered off again

in broad loops and sweeps through the skies
and out of sight brushed
stars in their going by atwinkle.

SAINT PETER'S COLLEGE LIBRARY
JERSEY CITY, NEW JERSEY 07306

The Stemless Flower

A big majestic poem, consummation,
could be written on the gradations
of flow from the gross to the fine:

but who would read it: no matter:
brevity's self-justifying: take
the energy of flow in diamonds,

rocks, trees, brooks, cyclones, in
light, feeling, mind, spirit:
of course, it's not just

the energy of flow, it's
constant energy operating in a
diminishing substance, so the sum

total of change in a diamond is
slight, but in a thought, how little
matter and how much speed: somebody

could hit the physicochemical texts
and come up with a nice rise on this
subject, a massive compilation and

registration, a book of order for the
disgruntled, misapplied times: and
motion would then sway all—as it does.

Imperialist

Everybody knows by now
that the weeds are mine
& knows I don't feel
altogether sorry for them:
but they I think
resent being owned or
written into roses.

Poem

In a high wind the
leaves don't
fall but fly
straight out of the
tree like birds

Imago

I refuse the breakage:
I hold on
to the insoluble knots
I've circled for years
turning in contradictory
wildness, as
safe with center as
jugs and stars: what
I can't become keeps me
to its image: what
can't be reconciled is
home steady at work.

Light Orders

Sometimes maple leaves come all of an angle,
stacked planes, resembling glimmery schools
of fish caught in dazzling turns: of course
leaves are a kind of fish the wind swims
its ocean through, and the glimmering—dislocated—

of a school might be no more than staid leaves
the ocean riffles like a wind: but a spider
out there on one leaf's built a surface web
over a lake of space, top of the leaf, stiffened
into a drought fold, sloop, and he's filtering out

whatever motion brings—the kill intended
exact, unglancing into metaphor: I feel
coming the rise of nets and flow and
the possibility of a further sea-wind summation
and many things have died since that was old.

History

The brine-sea coupling
of the original
glutinous molecules

preserves itself all
the way up into our
immediate breaths:

we are the past
alive in its
truest telling:

while we carry it,
we're the whole
reading out of consequence:

history is a blank.

Self-Projection

The driest place in the yard's
under the faucet:
where there is hose,
length will move
the source away
from its own critical drought:
hesitate and
undo: unscrew
and turn the undisciplined faucet
on: what more than the self
sometimes needs the self.

Outside-the-Household Hint

When picking
pears
off a hanging
pear-limb
start picking at
your highest
reach
and then pick
down into
the limb's rise:

If you start
picking
from
the bottom the
limb in
rising
will bear
the high pears beyond
you.

Metaphysic

Because I am
here I am
(nowhere)
else

Tussock

From high
winds the gulls
lie low: as the self

crouches from the
ragings of its
high mind:

hunkers down
into all that
silence can advise.

The Make

How I wish great poems could be written about nothing
you know just sitting around a comet coming
leaves falling off a bush in a cliff
ducks flicking their tails, a driblet spray,
the universe turning over or inside out
small prominences in the ocean wind-smoothed into waxen scallops
how I wish there could be the most exciting line ever going nowhere
or traveling making money spending it messing around
a warp in pure space just a warp unwarping
a stone losing three molecules into a brook's edge
or the point of a leaf trying to fall off by itself
how I wish that instead of poetic tensions there could be dreaming
shales of mind spilling off (with a little dust rising) into deep cones
a gathering and spinning out
into threads some so fine the mind rescues them with imagination
little bits of lightning when the wind bends them through the light
how I wish there could be such poems
about nothing doing nothing

Juice

I'm stuck with the infinity thing
again this morning: a skinny
inexpressible syrup, finer than light,
everywhere present: the cobweb becoming
visible with dust and the tumblelint
stalled in the corner seem worthy.

Terminations

Sometimes the celestial syrup slows
into vines
stumps, rock slopes,
it's amazing in fact how
slow it can get—diamond:

but then sometimes it flows
free in a flood
and high
so procedure drowns out
perception

practically, a roof showing
here and there
or a branch
bobbing:
as skinny

wind it recalls
and promises everything
but delivers nothing

except the song that
skims the mountains

and makes no sense
(except all sense)
to us
slowed discrete
out of following.

Fundamental Constant

The clouds,
from what possible formations,
nudged and shaped
to what directions,
came this
way
and the rain, hardly breaking
free from the
larger motions,
occurred:

I look through the window now
to the hedge
leaf
unsettled by a drop
that quivering to fall
blinks a prismatic
code
several kinds
of change sorting
through eons have
failed to change or break.

Making It

Entering the dark sounds
all right
if promising radical
loss of diversion
and going down into
dwelling through the dark
that sounds okay a
deepening into profundity
but at the giving
up into the dark of the dark
the loss of
the sight of sightlessness
a cry begins
to tear
that tears till it tears free

Scope

Getting little
poems off (clusters
of them) hits
centers—if lesser centers—
quicker and
set-wise like the rocks
of kaleidoscopes
makes infinite
combinations possible whereas
the long job's
demand for consistency
levels,
though the one center it
shoots for
may be deeper
(if hit
or if not moved away into
disintegration
by the fulsome carriages)

Weight

He loved cloud covers,
went into woods
to hide from stars: he
wept under bridges,
noticed weeds, counted
frog calls
till a stone in
his belly hardened
against infinity, the
grievances of levitation.

Ballad

I want to know the unity in all things and the difference
between one thing and another
    I said to the willow
and asked what it wanted to know: the willow said it
wanted to know how to get rid of the wateroak
that was throwing it into shade every afternoon at 4 o'clock:
      that is a real problem I said I suppose
and the willow, once started, went right on saying
I can't take you for a friend because while you must
be interested in willowness, which you could find nowhere
    better than right here,
      I'll bet you're just as interested in wateroakness
which you can find in a pure form right over there,
a pure form of evil and death to me:
I know I said I want to be friends with you both but the
willow sloughed into a deep grief
and said
if you could just tie back some of those oak branches
until I can get a little closer to mastering that domain
of space up there—see it? how empty it is
and how full of light:
      why I said don't I ask the wateroak if he would mind
withholding himself until you're more nearly even: after
all I said you are both trees and you both need water and

light and space to unfold into, surely the wateroak will
understand that commonness:
     not so you could tell it, said the willow:
        that I said is cynical and uncooperative: what could
you give the wateroak in return for his withholding:
what could I give him, said the willow, nothing
that he hasn't already taken:
     well, I said, but does he know about the unity in
all things, does he understand that all things have a
common source and end: if he could be made
to see that rather deeply, don't you think he might
        give you a little way:
     no said the willow he'd be afraid I would take all:
would you I said:
or would you, should the need come, give him a little way
back:
        I would said the willow but my need is greater than
his
and the trade would not be fair:
maybe not I said but let's approach him with our powerful
concept that all things arc in all
     and see if he will bc moved

Three Travelogues

I.

Off backwoods macadam
swinging back at a sharp angle
onto the sandy road
downwoods
laurel in hung cloud clumps opening
the sprung anthers
ready to shoot loose
multitudinous into the air
floats of pollen
gazes of yellow along the pinkribbed floral bowls:
a grouse hen
sanding
in sun at the road's edge,
not stirring, enthralled,
interruption
a disbelief,
the car's motion safety enough
and on along the ribbed rubbling road
to the white small bridge
at the turn's downward curve:
got out to see,
saw on the stream's bank

in full sun
the arching fern, its
cinnamon
rod lifting high, set off,
tall and honest,
waterbeetles swimming upstream,
darting, "standing" in flow:
on the other side
damselflies, blackwinged,
needle bodies
enameled, oriental green,
at the wingtips, strutted open,
a white dot, star,
the wings closed upward,
drawn open downward four white stars,
the lacy pumping of
amazement and desire

II.

Fell ashore in high seas,
the blackwet, weed-slickened canes of my raft
loosened by the surf approach:
rose between rocks and hit ground
beyond the sea's way:
held an armful of reeds from my breaking ship:
gleaned from swell and foam
slack straws to keep:

and went higher among sprayless rocks and stiff shrubs
and rested,

the stars available, multitudinous, the dark
wide, deeper than sight:

I lived there, treasuring
the rainpool in the scalloped rock,
stretching my clothes to showers, gathering
rain,
wringing the pool full,
drinking from the twisted fountain:

there I lived, preying
on gulls' nests,
splashing minnows from the runlets of caves,
sleeping,
the straws of my ship bedded under
stones from the wind's lift, dreaming,

tomorrow wings,
the cautious, off-circling eyes,
the water clear, dotless far as light
into the tunnels of rock,
fire's simmering,
a white-sailed cloud's blue hull of rain:

nude, brush-burned, alone: underwater, land and
vegetation, hostile, oily luxuriance,
the deep, windless surges, quiet, proliferation:
sang on the moon-bleached highest rock

the bell-less hours of night,
time-starved in the plenty of time

III.

An interruption makes a world: descent of
energies, failure of equilibrium: an unevenness,
imbalance:

in late March I went for a walk along the
margin of fields and woods
(margins are places for things to happen:
a line of difference there, disparity,
discernible change)
and could hardly bear the sight of the small events
happening in fullness, occurrences of promise or terror:
a green flake of weed between two larger flakes,
the dark wet ground clumpy, rising here or falling,
weed leaf curling to crowd into the sun,
that great body, furious and radiant, relating
directly to billions of events
too common to notice or too small: wild
plum blooming under the edge of pines,
a hold of ground and grass
saved along the ditchbank from the spring plow,

the extra green in a rye blade where a rabbit dropped
dark pellets (leaching out and lightening
to rain and sun): the placement

and width of brackets on a soggy stump:
these events:
I can hardly tell about them: they seem so
worthless yet are undiminished: so independent,
throwing back our meanings:

and followed the ditch down the wood's edge,
across the bottomland field, and
into the woods at the other side
and on down through the woods to where
in the branch the small ditch-flow lost
its separate saying: found a dry, high log, held
from the ground by the circle of turf it turned
in falling, and sat down
to see if I could take on the center of a filled out
world but heard from another fallen tree
a branch-trickle whose small music
from breakage and hindrance brought the world
whole and full again and to itself.

Sight Unseen

Take some prose and build
fairly shabby metrical dikes
around it, so it seems
firm enough, if empty, like

scaffolding (that was an
unintentional rhyme) and
(also unintentional) you have
a good representation of

the frame (pun unintended)
of mind most of us prefer—
at least, adopt: (here
see visions of people

like tendrils forming into
trellises growing up into
(unintentional) crane-like
triangulations, noble structures

that attain workable loft:)
nobody needs, apparently, or

apparently desires monstrous
extrusions of energy,

maniacal spools, jungle growths
of ascendancy that could
crunch the held spaces and
finger, in wobbly failures,

the sky (the sky of sky and
sky of mind): I am against
something but I don't know
what: failure, a fatigue

of the metal (or bracket loose),
enters into every means and
proposition, just as some little
success can be expected nearly

anywhere: I have no beef:
take a fairly unselfconscious
prose style, in a prosy day,
and fail to get excited

about its median flaws and
flows and sort of relax
into an adequate object: the
privileged moments confine

their privilege to moments

while we have to live, somehow,
all day: well, here we are, unlost,
advanced beyond being found:

there in the mirror is
a half-engaged willingness
to comply, an interest
we can practically claim.

Facing

I take your hand:
I touch your
hair, as if

you were going away
to be a long time
away, as

you must someday go
forever away:
lust burns out high

into light: I walk
away and back: I
touch your hair.

Glass Globe

I woke up (merely) and found
myself
inside a bulb of pain:
I said
everybody else looks all right,
it must be mine:
I kept it & kept it
shined invisibly clear.

Separations

Looking for clear water he
came from murky lowlands
to the desert and
after high plains & higher mesas

saw a white mountain
and going up into the sharp reaches

fell down and drank melt:
the cold water bore no
dream: he perished,
swilling purity.

Circling

Occurrence is continuous (and in
continuum)

(mind
ever making) and unmaking: the star
burns to the brim:
water moves:

motion organizes, parallel motions
echo along
parallels
and break out (or are broken out)
to oppose
other motions, confluences:

the white flakes of
rue anemone
spindled up
break into light

and broken

snow
against a surf of motions: (occurrence
continuous) and in
continuum.

Fix

Stumped again, I
sit and radiate
loss like
the message finally
come:

in truth, though, I
don't know what
to do: if
there were any

way out of this,
I'd, giving up
the sphere,
assume the linear,
smart as a bullet.

Weather

Guilt's been circling
my head all morning
waiting for the crime

to be defined
so conscience can drop
and punish the black meat out:

but all morning I haven't been able
to conjure up a single
wrong: the vulture rides

in the fairest weather:
light and warmth
send him higher, abler.

Coward

Bravery runs in my family.

Crying Out

Cool peripheries, raw
interludes of hedgerows,
confusions of ditchbanks,
brush weedstalks
standing: testing the mesh
for a rupture, I
trouble the rims
and distances of possibility
because
my center is vacant,
its hallelujah in a shambles.

Certainty

I have certainly felt the documentation of terror:
I have certainly known my
insides to turn all hands
and rush to the surface for help
and felt the hands go loose:
I certainly have come to believe in death;
my head rustles with footnotes and
quotation marks
that pinpoint places where my blood
has certainly stopped cold and certainly raced.

The Flaw

I never saw anything like it--
such a day:
coolish, dry, bright,
the sky deep blue,
trees and bushes a hard
dark green:
now
an hour before sundown
were it not
for the robin's song
rippling out along the pear limb
everything would be glass.

Triplet

Iris leaves
threes-in-one
cut
broadside into sun and rain
to send high
flop loose the
hairy huzzy
iris bloom

Design

It's actually six-thirty:
we've already been to
Scotch Hall for dinner:
I had tired flounder,
the whitest meat, in
every flake
extremest finery of black
lace, once bloodways:
now of course the
flounder has
completely foundered.

Rocking

The cock sparrow with a sweet
tweetering
did it on-and-off
fluttering four times quick
on the porch eaves:
the hen sparrow seemed
moved no further than
injunction's
"propagate the species:"
well, the sun's breaking
out, maybe she'll like that,
or maybe she means her
propriety to send
that earnest little
rooster off again.

Ars Poetica

The gods (for
whom I work) are
refreshing realists:

they let you into
paradise (which is
the best pay—

and pay they
know's the best
equalizer,

disobliging
all concerned)
and say, sing:

that's all: they
have their own
business: and

you can't begin
by saying, I've

been in

Hudson, Partisan,
and *Poetry:* the
gods are

jealous of their
own judgment: and
you can't say, I

feel sort of
stove-up today, just
got rejected

by *Epoch:* the
gods, as with other
species, don't give

a damn about
you, only the song,
and song is all

protects you there:
tough: but the
pay is good enough.

Course Discourse

Brief histories, scribblings,
are permitted to snow:
in winter woods, the
trees generous with open ground,
the parchment gets
through and, settling, sheets
the leaves:
and there's the legibility,
clumps of rabbit tracks
tracing through the trees,
the leap off a mound
onto the frozen, snow-hidden
puddle, the broad skid,
the skirmish of recovery
and the clumps again.

Obtrusion

The leaf has to be thick
enough to catch the light
and thin enough

to let it through:
the double governance, bind,
leads to precise adjustments,

optimum advantages within
constraining and releasing
possibilities: reason,

caught between holding to
know and letting go,
adjusts to the exact taint,

introducing into the medium
just so much of itself as
will construe but not destroy

the essence it seeks:
limit against limit
plays accuracy into procedure.

Louise

I drove down to Aurora
at 4:15 and picked up
Louise from work
and Louise's hair, what a deposit,
and her eyelashes and teeth,
her shoulders hung
with all that seemed to be
getting away with her sweater,
and I suggested McDonald's
for dinner but thought we
should stop off somewhere
first and get it over with:
Louise and I love relaxed
dinners and that's the
kind we had: Louise's
shiny fingers pulled
french fries out and her
stomach and hips and thighs
appreciated the hamburger: by
then I was feeling real loose
and easy and thought as we
left of Louise's ankles and

toes getting her out of the
place and of the way her
mind put it all together
without even thinking.

80-Proof

A fifth of me's me:
the rest's chaser:
35 lbs.'s
my true self: but
chuck 10 lbs. or so for bones,
what's left's
steaks & chops &
chicken fat,
two-over-easy & cream-on-the-side:
strip off a sheath of hide,
strip out nerves & veins
& permeable membranes,
what's left's a greasy spot:
the question's
whether
to retain
the shallow stain
or go 100% spiritual
and fifth by fifth
achieve a whole,
highly transcendental.

Having to Do with Birth

I've always been impressed with the word *incunabulum:*
even put a little off: *cun* immediately seems to be working
up to something—a kind of dash of feeling: and then

in cun suggests an actually ruffling stress or imminence
hard to turn back on: *nab*, however, seems practically
imperative, following so close upon, as if ready will

were enduring the nudges of insistent, jabbing impulse: but
then *nab u* personifies the thing out of figurative reason,
activating recall of a clutter of ideal images, set in

glow: *bul* is only an *l* short of the ideal presence of my
own hope in the piece: but I don't know that I like to be
stirred where I'd counted on the safety of lexical drought:

a *p* would complete *lum* to the afterwards feeling all
too puzzlingly well; the lassitude and disorientation
that while blessing the magic are half-relieved it's gone.

Limp Lump

Glubgullies in the fricassee:
careful: circling things are
out: terminals, too, scare me & I'm
alarmed at the coils beginnings imply:
let's shove one
another:
impotence comes when need
exceeds seed: much is needed here:
one feels overworked working over
the same old worked over work.

Mind

After the complex reductions come
the simple reductions, the apple
firm in the hand, weightless in the mind,

the elms drifted out of their roots, strung
into a green-wind wear, a sense of
seeing through never ending

in the endings, a piling into the sun
of the mind's sun returned: and then,
high with reductions, the chill that

we live where we can't live but
live there if we live, a house of mind
we never quite get the door open to.

Attenuations

Fantasies that do test the periphery of consciousness
let us have then, if death's the solid center absolute
but death's not, the center as much in the rufflings

of nothingness as the peripheries: for example, rock,
whole ragged ranges, that fells us with surficial weight,
weighs at the center of the earth nothing, becomes

outward flotation cast into poise by its opposite
radial: whichever way we move from the exact, we become
less like the local but more like the sphere: this

morning I turned a disintegrating ray on myself and
glimmered into mist, broke down further into limelight
and then became nothingness, continuum transportable.

Turning

From reality's flowing flurry
take out a glass bead
and steer round &
round
it, an everlasting:
the center's in there,
its invisibility seen through.

Swipe

In the useless study of uselessness one
gets cramps, twinges of contradiction—
how spiritless, in a sense, that contradiction
leads to wholeness, perhaps wholesomeness,
in that if anything can be presumed to have
been divided, contradiction can seem to be

taking both quotients into account: how
quickly uselessness makes a useful comment
on usefulness; for example, that mere usefulness
is useless, the useless less available
to the hacking divisions of definition,
a positive value: everything pays off a little.

Paradise

Rot richness, sticky, feverish,
that clears and thins, worm-gum globs
rinsing in rain,
the ripe garbage truck, odors
lacing the wind,
dispersing, molecule standing miles downwind
from molecule,
naked, odorless—the translation:
the mind has seen a clear place
beyond the reach of any molecule.

Satisfaction

Still I'm for upper
buzzardry: the high
easy fix
of the actual meal:
hunger lofts:
descent's a nasty dinner.

The Unmirroring Peak

What changes:
the changeable which
everything, including

the universe swelling
and shrinking from
bang to

bang, is: but
a summit in the
mind

holds expansion &
contraction to its
lesser heights,

changelessly out-and-in even there:
but in
the highest heights

where the converging loft
reaches past

material's finest

wash to immaterial
staying,
a land, the mind's,

where nothing comes
to pass,
lies, abides, untouchable

and unyielding:
down the slopes
changeable forms and colors

assume their fictions,
dread, joy,
despair but lie, press against

the rise whose angle
is invariant and whose
completion is final.

Pray Without Ceasing

I hear the low falling from the
highlands of hog-pasture, a music
of spheres, a couple: whatever is

done is to be
undone:
call me down from the
high places: I have achieved much
of the difficulty of my translation:

> stock in trade
> gunstock
>   stockings
>   stocks & bonds & good
>   stock
> put no stock in that
>   a stock case
>   in stock
>   stock the soup

3, the mystical figure, comes through:
the alternating, suspended,
opposing spheres undirected and

the directed unity, reconciler and
putter to sleep—
milt on
the levees of rationality:

    "O Aegypte,
Aegypte, of thy religious rites nought
will survive but tales
which thy children's children
will not believe;
nought
will survive but words graven upon
stones that tell of thy piety."
               (Trismegistus)

and in sleep, as in a natural sleep,
prone, face turned as if into breath,
he had about him needments, bottles of
rare glass, bowls: we wrapped him
in reed mat, rose from decomposing,
generating waters, went up on
the plateau
and put him in
sand: hereafter has
not changed since for him:
but his head's
magnificence and funny-stuff, those
epicycles of motion, rituals of
turning, dancing, the wind
has taken, nothing

changed into grass: all the way
out of the rise and fall:

O Egypt I sometimes hear the
future of the universe
speaking in a moonwheel's
turning of sand and light:

we set out a withe of silver grass and
it remains: it
has interfered with the natural wind,
fractured the paralleleity of
moonbeams and disturbed
lesser sandstorms: mimicry
so often far more succeeds:

you heal back from napalm: the
flame-scars pull chin to chest,
the fingers stick: the mercy
of sand's
scarless:

when the sand roars, a lion
rouses in the center, his eyes,
as if in a hollow, headless:
recognition is
the fiercest imperative:

a pararox, couple achers: the
real estate of the imagination:

whatever is—
terror, pity, grief, death,
rising—a child sits in explosion's
clutter, homeless, his small

driftwood legs, his eyes inventing
an equal rage & dark, white smears
of burn
the mask
his face must fit:
whatever is, brutality, the inner siege,
the mind orange, blue with
desolation's mold, something
thin & high
cuts through whatever is
and makes no difference of difference:

my mouth, become eyes, weeps
words: words spill
into
hyacinths: for my acquaintance
with grief is
intimate, lost voices my credentials:
singing's been sung: the same
body is crying:

fatigues snagged by wire,
bodies sag in their buttons, collars
flutter, surf jogs, the wind
all outside and usual:
blue dusk fills up under the gold smoke:
the sky violates nothing to intercede:

I held her
by the rose and
intruded: the petals
slickened, silken: I shaved

my head &
offered it there:
O rose
the microflora along your hinder walls
are fast bloomers: tunnel-scapes
beady with stiff
moss: who keeps the saltsea keeps
its plankton, not reasonable?
microflora, reproducing, don't mind
the long glider that
coming shoulders out the wind to
fundamental suction: collapsible
I live with
spherical walls:
everyway I look leaning in, leaning in's
the style &
passing over: I pick pockets of
perse pansies, poesies, posepays,
powder palls & wary:

I had a little pony:
his name was Dapple Gray:
and every time I had him,
he tried to get away:

who will eat from such a garden
let him have an oedipal situation
and my rights and privileges:

that the triadic Hegel could have been
evidencing his
genitals is a notion of

such cracking solemnity
birds fail to fly:

some are spring harvests: today,
April Fools', a squirrel in the leafless
elm gathered torn bark and inner tissue
from dead branches, wadding them
into her mouth then going limb by
thinning limb to leap onto the heavy
electric wire, then going upstreet to my
neighbor's streetside spruce: I
think that's
where the nest will be:
waste assimilated into
use: the result a neatness
unpremeditated, a re-ingestion of
process:
so arranged it is that my wasted
life becomes words
that through complexity and
unstructured swirl
seek the fall-out of
comparable enhancements:

occurrences
   recognitions
      surroundings

                  tensions sprung free
                  into event

happenstance & necessity

prediction & surprise
    moment & forever

and the gloomy, oh the melancholy,
remorseful
falling back and away
of time-sunk persons and places,
ragged knots
of a grounded, celestial kite:

yesterday robins
on the dark edge of dusk sang like
peepers:
I went out to listen
and they were robins:

and on the cold edge of spring
though on a warm day
we went out into the woods for
hepaticas up
along Six Mile Creek: we
found one spring-beauty and
by sun-warmed logs
a few clusters of hepatica,
hundreds of plants
but few bloomers: the
backfall of creekwater was
interesting, countercaps, and
compensating, the up-creek water
along eddying banks:

peripheries:

the dance about the fire,
utterance of tongues,
parlance of feet:
griefs can't be removed,
only altered, caught up into the
timed motions
of bearable sway:

fall in love with yourself
where it's shallow:
don't
thwart shriveling up by
suddenly drowning:

if change is certain, as say so many,
certainty is where there isn't any:

             pop gun
        soda pop
             pop art
             popsicle
        mom & pop
             popinjay
             pop in
             popeyed
             population

I can't get that star carted I said:
flooded carburetor, cracked voltage
regulator: I didn't realize at once
it was apt: a Starchief: and
one day a man said looking at
the dash word, it has

your name in it: *Starchief*:   he
was a good abstractor:

I had a little pony:
his name was Dapple Gray:
and when I tried to trim him,
he had a lot to bray:

an inch of snow last night but
mid morning is bright and melting:
the shadows are white:

napalm isn't falling here:
so what is it:

first, an explosion near the ground:
then a tarry rain,
soft and afire, falls, crumbles, & sticks:
sticks to trees, houses, children,
things like that: if
it hits it's 94.3% effective:

I see my death, my horror, the radical,
real, senseless pain,
as a coming afloat,
rocking in a mastery of oceans:
what time caricatures should
time keep:
to those busy making themselves
great, with grave music and
solemn looks, a thorough using up and

setting forth of language's materials,
I send
empty statements, slip-shoddiness,
incredible breeziness and such:
the wind we go to
understands everything:
I sing, though, in a way, the best I can,
for I may be understood
where I do not understand:

around the aureola matters get touchy:

confusion erodes the ice-glass
steel offices buildings of rationality:
anti-rationality only makes another
kind of thrust: complexity
blurs the sleek towers, wilts the
phallus of mistaken direction:

welcome to your unattended,
coin-operated, do-it-yourself
laundry:
bring and use your favorite bleach,
soap, and starch: if
machine is
defective, please use another machine:
to start washer put money in coin meter
and
(1) if slide type meter—slowly push
slide all the way in: then slowly
pull slide all the way out:

(2) if rotary knob type meter—
turn knob:
tub
will start filling not later than ½
minute after operating coin slide:

                stopcock
                        cock & bull
                ears cocked
                        cocktail
                peacock
                        cockle
                        cockney
                        cockiness
                        cockscomb
                poppycock
                        cockeyed
                        cockroach
                        cockpit
                        cocksure

dryclean wash 'n wears, even cotton
items: use this
handy clothing guide: follow
these simple steps:
brush away loose lint
and other soiling matter: turn sweaters
inside out: turn down cuffs of
trousers: insert the

necessary coins:

rubbers, after several drycleanings,
tend to lose elasticity: plastic-coated
fabrics often become stiff.
beware sequins, beads, and other fragile
ornaments, can get you into trouble:

remove wear wrinkles and sharpen creases
and pleats: some spots refuse
to come out, rust, mildew, dried paint,
indelible ink:

little artery, couple inches long,
branching into cardiac muscle: it pops
and you give up philosophy and
ultimate concern, car payments, son and wife,
you give up the majors & minors,
the way you like your egg cooked, your
class ring, lawn,
sparrows nesting in the garage, the
four crocus bulbs (maybe more next
year), toenails and fillings:

I wouldn't want to happen up on any
critters of eternity, absolutes that
end the world: fellow said one star
up there in our galaxy is mostly
gadolinium, a rare earth;

nobody knows how the concentration occurred:
then there are other surpluses and
scarcities
that uneven the tissue:
I wouldn't want anything
to get known tight: ignorance is our
boat giving us motion: or, capsized,
knowledge is our ark which is more in
line with the tradition:
  the ocean would then
  be what it
  is:

spirit, though
it encompasseth mightiness, etc., however,
cannot, like a motor,
raise and lower
toast:

nothing matters, believe me, except
everything: to sift & sort, magnify
& diminish, admit & renounce, impairs
the event:
what the mind can't accept's obscene:
the rest shines with an
additional, redeeming
light,
the light in the head
of language in motion:

the wave coming in, running, gathers,

lofts, curls—the instant of
motion's maximum
organization: then: then one is
forty & hollow: the curl's reach
redeems the hollow, equals it, till
the curl touches over: what is the
use: the crashing, the hollow coming
topside into wide prevalence,
the flat waters skinnying out and
rushing back—is merely endurance
until the next wave lifts:
as for what's left,
dip it and ship it: to have made
it here is not to have it made:

entering is lovely:
such delicacies, scents, the
feminine source, perfumes: cookies
in the oven, delights:

mixmaster, mixmaster,
mast me a mix, ur,
mix me a mist, ur . . .
the mixers and blenders chew up
differences: chomp & whirl
to knotless paste: the spurt for
equilibrium:
to compensate for which somewhere root,
bark, leaf must make a walnut, some
skinny saint rail through the cosmos,
shot from earth by penury and dread:

what is more costly or
needed than a mind shot to space by
shiny thrust, a renunciation of
earth, a negative blast away:

I have seen all the way in with
a white bang that they
are spheres, round solids, sprinkled,
lightly, in a medium, not
empty, called space and that
these round bodies go round
different orders of center
that swoosh away burning
their peripheries and sucking
their centers through virgin space, neither
up nor
down—the
terror that that is
the way it is,
that particular way, a
pure flower of terror:

ancient souls sitting on
the bright banks of forever
in
raptures of old acquaintance: for every
never again,
an always again: and young souls
from their quick missing
quick as branches and glittering:

where the lost remains, immortal in
the foreverness of the lost:
say good morning, say buon giorno,
say hi
to infant brother, to mother, father,
sit down under the golden pines on
the slopes of no further parting:

the Buddhist nun burns for the peace
her ashes will achieve:

the village woman coming home finds
her shack afire, her
son & husband shot: she bends down
where she is:
she is given tokens of the dead but
her left arm like a sickle reaps at the
air
for the harvest
already taken:

through the reeds somewhere, as by a
paddy or ditch in her head,
wind burrs
a leaf: the woman flutters,
her grief absolute and
not a mystery:

how can I know I
am not

trying to know my way into feeling
as

feeling
tries to feel its way into knowing:
it's
indifferent what I say: the motions
by which
I move
manifest
merely a deeper congruence
where the structures are:

run my poem through your life and
exist, decommissioned,
like rubble,
innocent, slouchy on the uptake:

the scramblers, grabbers, builders—
rubblerousers: sticking stone to
false stone in a unity of walls which
wants to come apart: let
weeds and grasses move in among a
scattering, make a little shade, hide
mice, give burrows to ground bees,
byway hideouts to the engines of spiders,
stones the
owl can come and sit in moonlight on:
we
should all be in a shambles, shacked up,

peeping round the grasshoppers,
preserving a respectful quiet:

don't snatch & grab: grab snatch:
laboratory tests attest,
when a system of two bodies
charges and discharges itself
it's peaceful as tulips:

can a 41-year-old man living on dandelion leaves
from the cool edges of junkyards
find
songlore enough
in the holocausts, boggy garbage,
fly swarms, lamb bones, and rust-floral
cans
of his weedy search
to sustain interest:

the continuum, one
and visionless, within
which
the breakdown of pure forms,
arising of skyscrapers, laws,
the high crystal-clear arising
of theory:

the evening blue-purple, the trees
black,
the birds can't quit singing: damp

heat built
and rose through the golden towered afternoon,

broke finally into motion, as of
descent, rain beating
straight down
between racks of thunder:

can anything be erased: can this day's
praising hold to the day it praises
down the slopes of total entropy:

pray without ceasing:

we found hailstones in the grass
and ate them to cool:
spurred stones
with interior milkwhite halos,
an arrested spangling:
the high hard water
melted
aching our tongues.

Saint Peter's University Library
Withdrawn